Aamir Dean Hassan is a Queer British South Asian. He is passionate about spirituality, chasing your happiness and continuing to heal on your journey in this life. Along with his husband, he hosts a successful podcast 'You Don't Love Me', all about life from the perspective of a gay, South Asian married couple. You can join Aamir in his life by following him on Instagram @shehzada_aamir_ and you can check out his life with his husband @youdontlovemeboys.

Copyright © Aamir Dean Hassan, 2023

Can I Escape My Mind?
by Aamir Dean Hassan
Paperback Edition

First Published in 2023 by

Inkfeathers Publishing
Vivek Vihar, New Delhi 110095
www.inkfeathers.com

ISBN 978-81-19483-50-1

All rights reserved. No part of this book may be reproduced, lent, resold, or transmitted in any form or by any means, electronic or mechanical, including photocopying, recording, or by any other information storage and retrieval system, without permission in writing from the publisher.

CAN I ESCAPE *my* MIND?

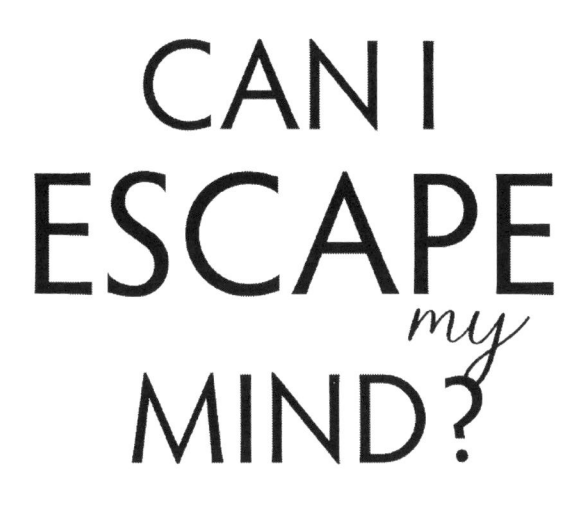

AAMIR DEAN HASSAN

Inkfeathers Publishing
www.inkfeathers.com

To every single person who has suffered.
To every single person trapped in their mind.
To every single person who is hurting.
This is for you.

Choose the light.
Choose your happiness.
Follow your destiny.

Contents

Preface   xi

Obscurity

1.	How?	1
2.	Existing	3
3.	What will I become?	4
4.	Gone Forever	6
5.	Hurting	9
6.	Wasted Torment	11
7.	Kill Me	13

Woeful Melancholy

8.	Broken	17
9.	Fire	18

10.	I Miss You	19
11.	Is survival worth it?	22
12.	Roll the Dice	23
13.	Pain	25
14.	False Glimmer	26

Torture

15.	RAGE	29
16.	My Head	30
17.	The Monster	32
18.	Energy	33
19.	Venom	36
20.	Weapon and Shield	38
21.	No Outlet	39

Unwavering Soul

22.	Written in the Sermon	43
23.	Louhi	48
24.	Four White Walls	50
25.	Darkness	51
26.	Put Me Out of My Misery	53
27.	It's Over	54
28.	Flatline	56

My Fate?

29.	Crescendo	61
30.	Linger	62
31.	Sadness	63
32.	You're Not Worth It	64
33.	Torchbearer	65
34.	I have No Purpose	66
35.	Hello	68

Embers

36.	Disappointment	71
37.	Discontinue	72
38.	I've Got This	74
39.	Rebirth	75
40.	The Place For Me	77
41.	Clarity	78
42.	Air	80

Dear me…

43.	Destiny	85
44.	Moon	86
45.	And still…I thrive	89
46.	Keepsake	90
47.	Purpose	91

48.	To Be Free	92
49.	Skin Deep	93

Lineage

50.	They Are Here	99
51.	Bigger	100
52.	Just Smile	101
53.	Motherland	102
54.	Home	103
55.	Devilish	104
56.	Our Power	105

Free Mind

57.	Awakened into Unconsciousness	109
58.	Universe	110
59.	A Path Not Too Far	111
60.	Presence	112
61.	Evolution	113
62.	Magic	114
63.	Thank you	115

Preface

This short anthology of poems and words was written over the course of years of adulthood: on and off. It was originally going to be around my tormented and suffering mind, but something told me to hold back sharing this with the world until I was fully ready as something was always missing.

The missing pieces fell into place in 2022/23 in which I had several spiritual awakenings, found my flow in this life, and followed the whispers of the universe into happiness. I want anyone reading to go through the journey of my mind and I want everyone to know that you are capable of living the life you want, and you are worthy of happiness.

Obscurity

How?

The Earth. The Moon. The Stars.

How did it all get here? I question this every day.

I question this so much that my brain hurts. That my skull shatters.

You see, I like answers. I can be a truth seeker and it is because the answers are out there.

How is it possible everything around us is here? I am here.

I taste. I hear. I see. But how?

Is someone really up there playing puppeteer with us? Laughing at us and mocking us.

Did something really big really bang? This is all unfathomable to me.

Then my heart starts to hurt and my body starts to shake.

This is when I think the outrageous things. Because it is outrageous that we are here.

Pause for a moment and have some time to think about it.

Then I think why? For what reason? To fight? To live? To survive?

What is my calling?

How did we become?

Existing

How are you supposed to live and be when you cannot be yourself?

How are you supposed to breathe when you are always suffocating?

Suffocating under something you cannot control.

Suffocating under something you do not know.

I do not understand this feeling.

I am so different, and I am so ashamed. A shambolic disgrace to anyone and everyone.

A disappointment beyond belief

Is there a point to my existence?

What will I become?

In this world you are told who you are supposed to be,
A man, a vessel, an enigma, controlled and contorted
for either happiness or sadness locked in a little box
tucked up inside your head.
The questions you ask yourself become monotonous
The questions you ask yourself become a strain on the
self-belief and desire you should have.

These questions float about until you break.
But what is 'breaking' when you aren't allowed to
crack?

When this 'breaking' will be beyond a weakness to those around you

'Community', 'Family', do I even know the meaning of these words?

Who am I?

What am I?

What will I become?

Gone Forever

Fag. Gay. You're a faggot. The screaming rings in my ears.
Take me to HELL and let me feel the embers burn through my skin.
Anywhere would be better than here.

I picture the fire wrapping like a warm blanket around me,
the comfort it gives me, the escape from the real world burns me to my core.

Lispy. You can't speak right. Pronounce your S's correctly.

I call upon the Evil beings, grab my legs and pull me down with you.

Rip me to pieces and swallow me up.

I see my bones shattering into tiny pieces,

I love the thrill and envy the vision.

My skull rolling on to the floor, void of all thoughts at last.

Dirty. You don't belong. Get away from me you FREAK!

When will I be good enough for the vision of others?

Drain the blood from my body and leave me to rot.

I do not want to do this anymore

It's time to create enough tears to drown in…

No message left,

No disappointment.

Hurting

———✦———

Hurting can be so much fun when you are addicted to the love,

As there is no love for yourself and you do not know how to find it.

Why is everything so chaotic? Disarray is not what I asked to be born into.

Disorder. Disaster. My mind needs to find sanctuary.

You cannot find sanctuary when every single place you look is full of malevolence.

Sin and immorality poison the streams that seep into this home,

tearing down the wallpaper that was tarnished by violence,

bringing in no joy, just more destruction and devastation.

I concede.

I cannot fathom anymore of this.

When will this hurt stop?

Wasted Torment

Do you know who you are?

Of course not...

I have no time to live, breathe, think, become...

It is constant GO

        GO

            GO

survival at all times, no time to slow down and no slowing down

Eloquent on the page but turmoil everywhere else

How can I think, no time for the questions, the frustration coming out of my fingertips writing this, the regrets, I should have become myself so so so long ago,

Wasted time, a wasted life,

I did not ask to be born into this cycle of abuse.

CRACK!

Head smashed on the wall.

I wake up barely in a pool of blood, what a shame, I have no choice to be a survivor…

A survivor is far from what I want to be…

A painless end is needed.

But I keep going

I kept going

Was it worth it?

Kill Me

Entering existence isn't as easy as it may seem.

Entering existence…is it even worthwhile?

Going through all the stages and phases,

Penetrating your mind and soul with so many obscure viewpoints…

> How do you find the correct path?
> What is the 'correct' path for a being like me?
> Misdirection, redirection, I just want direction…

Entering existence should be full of love and praise.

Not the fear of putting a foot wrong…

'Wrong' in the eyes of others…not in lawful terms.

Not the fear of feeling the thud on your back

The slap across your face

The kick to your stomach

                                      For living

                                              For existing

No wonder I don't want to exist anymore.

Woeful Melancholy

Broken

My heart.

The poor thing.

It's been broken so many times.

Never by a lover.

By a friend.

By a confidant.

By blood.

By my memories.

By my reality.

Fire

Flames

Embers

Burn me

Take me whole, swallow me up and spit me out so everyone can see the scraps of me left.

I Miss You

I miss you

What do I miss?

The trauma haunts me

Dealing with it is a daily routine

But I miss something

I miss what I never had

I miss what it was supposed to be

I miss the laughter

But it always had undertones

Any light and great moment

I knew I was going to lose it all

At what cost?

I can't live another way

But I miss you

Miss you all so much at times

That I must repress every single feeling inside me

I tell the world it's ok, it's not

It makes it easier for me and for everyone

I am the shoulder to cry on

Not the other way, ever

I am strong

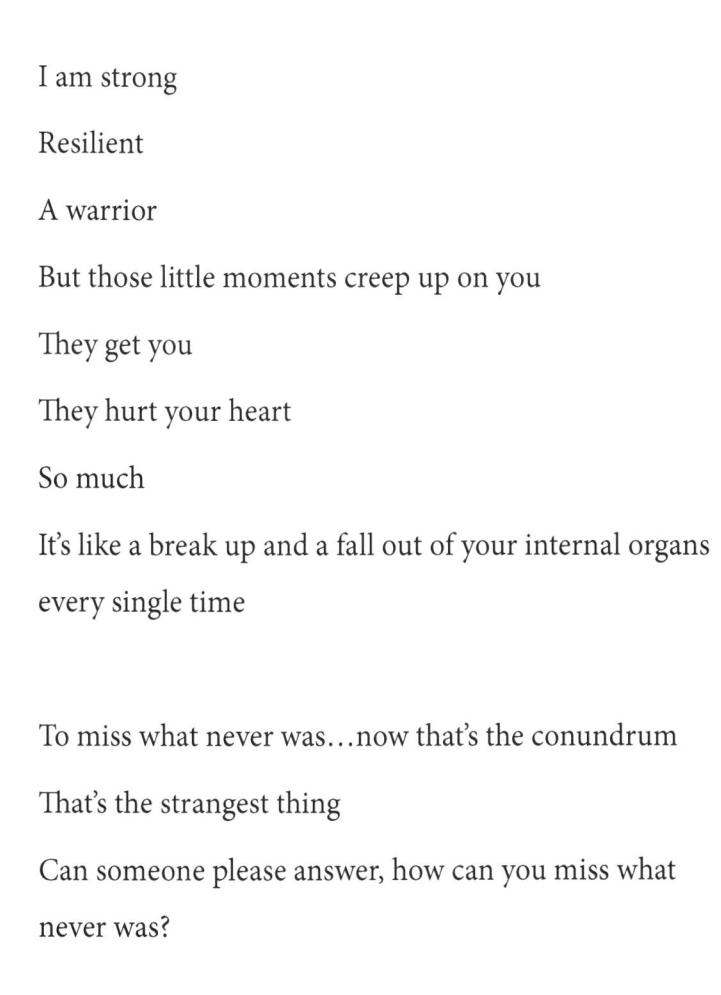

Resilient

A warrior

But those little moments creep up on you

They get you

They hurt your heart

So much

It's like a break up and a fall out of your internal organs every single time

To miss what never was…now that's the conundrum

That's the strangest thing

Can someone please answer, how can you miss what never was?

Is survival worth it?

———✧———

Did I ever think growing up that this would be my life?

I woke up one night shaking and everything flashed by.

Tears streaming down my face; trembling uncontrollably.

It's like I had been asleep and had just pushed through.

As though I had numbed myself to survive.

Roll the Dice

Ever felt as though you were shedding skin?
As though your evolution was excruciating.
Do you play safe and drown in monotony?
Do you risk it all and play a game of jeopardy?

Exhaustion and mental anguish are the number one enemy.
How do you eliminate this from your life?
Can you ever eliminate this from your world?
The goal is to blossom and prosper.

Questions build and build.

Never answered.

You hold the control and the power.

What to do?

Shall I roll the dice?

Pain

Why was I robbed?

Why me?

I didn't want to be dealt this hand, please pass it on to someone else. I'm not evil, not bad, yet still have this difficult hand of cards.

I force myself to soar so high and it's so I don't have to see what's on the ground, to delve into what was and what it was like. The pain cannot be destroyed. The pain always lingers underneath. The paint doesn't haunt me, instead it has become a part of me.

False Glimmer

I see it in your eyes.

That little glimmer.

You're not happy.

That glimmer is false.

You're hurting.

Hurting so much.

Embrace the hurt.

It's the only way to heal.

Torture

RAGE

Have you ever felt so much rage? So much rage that has no place anywhere and you do not know where to place it? So much rage that crying in the shower is the heaven in your life? Have you ever wanted to hurt the air around you because you simply do not know what to do? The ball of fire inside of you teasing you and yet you survive the embers. The ball of fire growing and growing desperate to be unleashed but you know when it is unleashed you will burn down everything around you. No survivors left. Nobody to tell the tale. The tale of the angry man. The tale of the man full of so much rage. The man that has no time to tackle and deal with the depths of trauma. Have you ever felt so much rage that you become so numb and cold against all the heat and burning? Have you ever felt so much rage that your insides die and you feel no pain?

My Head

Fuck fuck FUCK FUCK FUCK
BLAHHHHHHHHHHHHHHHHHHHHHH
JUST SIMPLY SHUT the fuck UP!

Why can't I shut it up? Why won't it stop? Deafening me on all accounts and abusing every ounce of me. JUST FUCKING STOP!

I claw my eyeballs out, pull out my hair, scratch my skull to pieces and take off every eyelash one by one, one by one, one by one, one by one, one by one, one by one, nobody can stop me, I cannot stop myself. I need serious help. Help from this infliction, is it even that anymore? I simply do not know.

My skull laid in tiny little shattered pieces and I start to pick at the skin on my body down to the flesh. Flesh spewing everywhere, I cannot fathom what I see before me but it is there and I cannot do anything about it.

My bones, finally I reach them. FUCK! STOP! STOP! STOP! There is still time to STOP! I can't.

I am stumped. Chaotic entanglement of my conscience.

Aamir Dean Hassan

The Monster

———✦———

Touch of the skin, preserve the moment.

That touch will always be a whisper on your heart.

The heart, so fragile, so gentle; be careful.

Tenderness is key.

Pressure the heart then you will pressure the mind.

You awake the monster living inside.

No regret when the monster breathes,

destroying everything, apologising for nothing.

All from one touch, one careful touch,

one delicate touch of a broken heart.

Be careful with that touch, it could ruin you.

Ruin your life and take over your being.

Energy

Give me the bat and ball and let me show you how it's done.

You don't believe I can do it but watch me go.

I don't miss.

I wait in the line until it is my turn,

I wait ever so patiently, and I am so excited to play.

I am like a child waiting for their mother to come home with sweets.

Sweat is trickling down my brow, my memories dart back to my youth.

Incredible to be reliving the summer moments with the same people,

this time I have everything crossed that my team will win.

I will make sure we win as I have become an excellent batter.

I never miss.

My turn now.

Finally. I get to do what I always wanted to.

I can rectify losing in my youth.

I take the bat.

A smash! Told you I wouldn't miss!

I run the distance from base to base as I hear the sirens in the distance.

I am smiling from ear to ear as I hear screaming and whaling.

'He's dead'

'You killed him'

I told you I wouldn't miss.

Venom

The manifestation of this monstrous beast knows no bounds,

It screams and shouts beneath my veins and it tears out my insides

without a moment's notice. I cannot scream in pain because it means

the voices in my head will know. The battle between these conflicts

are never ending. My body, my mind, who or what will prevail?

The beast knows the tatters that lurk under my skin and the scars

I hold so close to my heart. He knows the bruises on every muscle and the pain I carry so heavily on my back. He kicks and punches at

every chance he gets, he comes to the surface and I bleed. The beckoning

voice in my mind knows of my tormented thoughts. It knows what I

want to do to myself when nobody is there. This voice knows the hate I hold.

This voice screams and shatters my eardrum to pieces.

It escapes and venom spews out.

Weapon and Shield

The immediate response is defensive and dangerous,

Don't dare come in my way because I will pounce on you.

I will pounce so hard you won't be able to breathe

I will pounce so hard you will wish to die.

I have become my own weapon and shield,

All you have to do is push me a little,

Push me ever so slightly,

And I will destroy you, detonate your life and refuse to pick up the pieces.

No Outlet

No outlet for the emotions inside.

No outlet to deter me from evil.

No outlet to deter me from my hatred.

Maybe I am lying to myself.

I shouldn't worry.

But I cannot see anything else.

Worry, shame, anger.

It's hard to decide. I want to take flight. I constantly lose control, what am I supposed to do?

Stay   On

Track   (I tell myself this)

Aamir Dean Hassan

On track may be stable.

But my stability isn't what you think.

It is warped.

My eyes bulge and my brain hurts.

I want to jump. I want it so bad. I want the depths of the oceans to enter my mouth and drown my lungs. Crush me. Devour me. Take me. Control is muted. Control is non existent.

Unwavering Soul

Written in the Sermon

I just wanted to feel the twist of fate,

Will they live or will they die?

Am I worthy of this power to decide?

I guess I am but sometimes I am doubtful,

I wonder why I doubt my rationality.

It all makes sense to me…

I love you.

So devilishly handsome and unflawed,

Your dark brown locks fall gracefully,

Your deep green eyes a portal,

A portal to perfection.

Infectious smile and radiating skin,

You ooze all the wonderous delights.

The eighth wonder. My only wonder.

My darling dear, why do you toss and turn so much?

Is it a nightmare you are having?

You must be possessing dark thoughts,

As I am harboring all the intellect.

Ah, you have calmed down now,

And allowed your beauty to prevail.

I worship your existence.

Lucifer made you in his honour.

Leviathan could not stand the creation.

They fought and fought.

Bloodshed in the sea.

Until Leviathan was decimated.

You did such a thing,

You are the blood of the fallen,

Azrael is waiting for you.

Your dream weaving will stop soon,

You will not enter another realm.

Your humanity has been a beautiful destruction,

Termination is imminent.

A love letter will take you into the afterlife…

Oh, my Eros,

How I have always been so encapsulated by your exquisite nature,

You pour your worldly desires into everything you do.

Your breath, your walk, your touch…my head spins just thinking.

This is torture and hell you are putting me through;

I love you enough to do it.

I do look forward to having a bond unmatched,

Those that Fairytales wish they could pen.

Perhaps our love, life and fatality shall be in poetry and prose one day.

Perhaps we will send hope to the future.

I love you.

Have the sweetest dreams and I shall be with you so very soon,

I am so blessed to be the provider and deliver your final sermon.

They say till death do us part, but I say death is merely just a part…

I wish you could see me beaming as I write this final message.

Goodbye, not for long and see you on the other side.

In hope I write.

Afraid, I am not.

I have the fortitude and courage,

But I pray to my heavenly fathers it works.

I take the knife and prick my finger.

Blood pours out, I know it shall work.

Can I Escape My Mind?

I take the knife far from my blissful heart,

Turn it on your body and deliver what is needed.

I sing Great is Thy Faithfulness as you squirm,

I wipe the tears away from you and look into your eyes.

I smile and stroke your hair as your insides revolt.

You are now in Paradise.

My Dear. My Love. Gone.

Louhi

I feel alone again and this time it is the worse it has ever been.

You built me up so much and shattered all my dreams with no remorse.

The path I am trying to go down is constantly broken and I continue to trip and fall.

Everyone around me is dismissive of the feelings I hold so I just carry on

But inside I am in excruciating pain, a pain I have never before felt.

Am I addicted to the pain? Do I enjoy this?

The only reason I question this is because you say I am married to the darkness.

Can I Escape My Mind?

She sits inside of me and she calls out my name.

Lingering seductively and ready to pounce.

Sniffing out my weaknesses to take advantage.

She is always here, and I always feel her presence.

Possessing the power of Louhi.

I am the imitation of Louhi in your mind.

Death, disease and decay are my true loves.

You are not married to me for I have never married.

I am not hurting you.

Dig deeper and deeper to find the cause of pain.

I have set my sons to wreak havoc on your mind.

The 9 deadly diseases that will cause disintegration.

Limb by limb.

I am destroyed.

Nobody cared to help.

Even through my screaming.

Aamir Dean Hassan

Four White Walls

———✦———

Panic. I can't cope.

Breathing. Doesn't exist.

It's over.

All over.

Nowhere to go.

Nowhere to escape.

Four walls as solitude.

Solitude?

Oh God.

Kill me.

Darkness

We watched the black clouds hover above,

Bleak and meek, patiently we stood.

Waited and waited, wishing the day away,

Hoping one day that all we would do was lay.

The voice inside my head was the other part of me,

Darkness had took over but nobody could see.

Her scent so strong, she wouldn't go away,

Hoping one day that all we would do was lay.

Aamir Dean Hassan

Infiltrating my being; what had I become?

I was nobody's lover; I was nobody's son.

She was punishing me, I tried to push her away,

Hoping one day that all we would do was lay.

We both now hoped and we both now wanted.

Finally, I lay. All my pain went away.

Patiently she stood and watched and watched,

Watched the black clouds hover above.

Put Me Out of My Misery

Suffocate me.

Strangle me.

Just get rid of me.

I will help you dispose of me.

Nobody will ever find out.

Please.

I beg you.

You owe me this at least.

Squeeze my insides out.

Show me I am nil.

Show me I am naught.

Show me I am zero.

Put me out of my misery.

It's Over

I cannot seem to find a way out of this emotion and feeling therefore I am hoping the sporadic moving of pen to paper, the scribblings and the ink splatted on all my pages will help me.

Have you ever built your hopes up so high and been promised the whole entire world? Yes, you say.

Have you ever had every single thing at reach to be ripped away from you? Yes, you say.

I would rather have my heart crushed.

I would rather have my nails ripped off.

I would rather have every single part of my being beaten up and battered until I cannot move any longer.

The pain is not subsiding, and I do not understand why. I tell myself that time is the greatest healer, but this time there seems to be no healing.

Time is moving but I am not. Time is escaping me. My heart beats so fast.

Oh no

What do I do

I have lost all form of coherence in my life

It's over.

Flatline

———✦———

I'm slipping away from this life,

a life I never truly entered.

My lips tremble and my blood runs cold,

what have I done…what have I become?

I wish I could say a shadow of my former self,

but that doesn't even come close…

there was no former self and I know that now.

I wish I could say I am out of control,

but that doesn't even come close…

Can I Escape My Mind?

I collapse.

I clutch my chest.

I feel my heart.

I finally feel my heart.

Flatline.

My Fate?

Crescendo

Waves soar and crash. Soar and crash.

These waves signify horror and torment. They will eat me alive.

It is a must to survive.

Survive.

Survive the drowning. Survive upsurge. The hurricane.

Twists and turns of the hurricane. Drowning in the water. Take me away.

Far away. Away from here.

To a land of no hurt; a land with sleep.

Sleep and rest.

Rest and silence.

Linger

Lingering scent, twirling around.

Captivating. Nauseating.

Entering our lungs; controlling our blood streams.

Escape…

How would we escape?

How had 'I' become a 'we'?

Lingering scent, taking over.

Allowing the corruption…

Allowing the hurt…

Enjoyment.

Lingering.

Tormenting.

We.

I.

Sadness

What does sadness mean to you?

Emptiness inside…nothing.

Floating and lingering with no force or presence.

No desire or willingness to stand your corner.

Giving up…

Insides hurting, burning and then- numb!

Numb at all.

Numb to everything.

No pieces to shatter.

Nothing.

But, why so sad? A reason undiscovered.

A reason above all reasons.

A reason you cannot reason with.

What does sadness mean to you?

You're Not Worth It

How can you tell me to calm down?

When you don't have to fight every day.

Fight just to exist.

Even breathing is a battle.

I owe you no explanation.

Your rhetoric speaks for itself.

Disappointed and disgusted.

You vile supremacist scum.

Torchbearer

I am the light.

I am my own light.

I am your light.

Is my light allowed to dim?

I want to be in darkness.

Enveloped in the darkness.

Allow the darkness to consume me.

Can someone else be the light?

Can someone else run with this torch?

I have No Purpose

———✦———

It follows me and it never, ever stops like this is my destiny.

I try to silence it and I try to move on. I improve, get better, give love and make sacrifice.

For what?

For my pre-determined fate to continue gnawing at my ankles and polluting my insides like some fucked up blotch that will never leave.

I park it, I give so much fucking love, time, patience and hold my tongue, for what?

Ultimate sorrow.

You squeezed every single last breath from me. Is this love?

My father was right to leave me.

I was broken the moment I was born, and my fate and destiny sealed.

What is my purpose if every time I rebuild and every time i give to others, I am shattered, I am broken, I am brought back down to reality.

Used. Nothing special. Another speck on this shit Earth, ready to swallow me whole and not even bother to spit me out again.

Hello

Hi,

It's me again.

I'm suffocating here.

I can't take it anymore.

Drowning in small minded talk.

Keeping my head down.

Avoiding eye contact.

I am only human after all.

Please stop my head thumping.

Please stop my chest tightening.

Please help me.

Thank you.

Embers

Disappointment

Harassment. Evil. Torture.

You tried to turn people away from me.

I thank you.

You showed me I don't need them.

I thrive better now.

I thrive on another level now.

The rest are dirt.

Pathetic excuses for friends.

Weak individuals.

So very toxic for me.

Not the energy I desire.

Discontinue

Sinister obscurity succeeding every crevice of my soul,

Truth unfolded; beating at the pace of my heart.

Confusion, perplexity and bewilderment.

Turning to loved ones- shunned away.

Holding expectations- shunned away.

Testing and strenuous times- poison heart.

Misinterpretation, miscalculations, mistakes- toxic heart.

Monuments of melancholy: goodbye, co'o , adeus.

Crossing the threshold of knowledge, questioning all.

My journey, not yours.

Be there.

Submission into my contemplations: hypocrisy, weakness and malevolent acts around.

Questioning- not acceptable.

Your insincerity sending shocks to my system,

The duplicity revealing the paleness in your heart.

Gold.

Gold, white, silver.

Purity. Smiles. No chains. No hypocrisy.

Truth put to bed.

Confusion, perplexity and moving forward.

Finding new loves ones.

Holding zero expectations.

Testing and strenuous times- honest heart.

Repositioning my vision, causing headaches and heartache.

Could a poison heart experience such hurt?

Could a poison heart experience such exhilaration?

Devotion. Adoration. Friendship.

All revealing the love and tenderness in my heart

I've Got This

Look in the mirror,

Tell yourself 'I've got this'.

Chase what you truly want,

Feel the weights lifting.

Every step you take,

Is a step closer to the taste you want.

The taste you deserve.

The taste that could unsettle people.

Take it.

Rebirth

Light causes the shadows to fall,

they chase me without hesitation.

I follow obscurities as the disinclination flows through my veins,

all the deceptions and slurs revealed.

Faster and faster,

light the fire and watch it burn.

Beaming as I examine the embers,

the past diminishing before me.

No warning signs,

crash and collapse.

The termination of contractual agreements,

the thrill now begins.

Exasperation combined with acceptance,

I witness everything in its entirety.

Finally flying without falling,

a defiant warrior is reborn.

The Place For Me

The place of dreams.

For me:

The place of acceptance.

The place where I am able to breathe.

The place I don't suffocate.

The place I don't have to pretend to be blind.

The place my voice is heard.

The place of dreams is simple just the place for me.

Clarity

Pick up the pieces and put the jigsaw back together.

Piece by piece, corner by corner, make it work.

Cut it up, force the edges, make it work.

Connect all the dots…it's dot to dot.

Force the image and picture it clearly.

Make it clear…really clear.

But mainly- make it work.

Eradicate anything that stops this from happening.

Eradicate any real sense and purpose.

Eradicate any pieces and dots that don't work,

As all you've got to do is make it work.

Don't question it- don't you dare!

Don't pause at all- show no weakness!

This is normality- like nothing to you…

Listen…and make it work.

Air

Feel it through your air and against your skin.

Allow yourself to lose control and feel light on your feet.

Look up into the sky and see the blue…smile…

Lay your head down on the sweet grass,

Make out the shapes in the clouds and breathe

In

And

Out

Breathe

Don't stop

Smile.

The blessed feeling of survival. The blessed feeling of being here.

You have so much left to do.

The candle isn't close to dimming. You are here. You can finally feel.

Dear Me...

Destiny

———※———

Clear as light; clear as day.

Dark as night; dark as your heart.

Choose a path and follow your Destiny.

Moon

Glistening.

Glistening through ecstasy. The shimmer of moonlight lingered. Dangerously it crept through the sky attempting to determine the direction in which it had a duty to move to. Progressing hesitantly; exceeding its limits. Ominous beams seducing the pale backdrop of nightfall.

What was the need for this presence? Why did it begin to loiter in the air?

The beams halted.

Cautiously they scanned their surroundings. Eagle eyed in search for their prey, their next victim perhaps? On they proceeded. Creating patterns up above, colliding into one another. Each and every beam stood strong: some delicate, some curious and some enraged.

Delicate. Swooning through the sky. Picturesque and passive. These exquisite beams lit up the world. Nobody was afraid. They were approachable and stunning. Zooming by one another in a refined fashion and greeting one another with joyous exasperation.

Curious. Lurking in the sky. Prying and probing. Yearning to know all the secrets of the world. These rays were meddlesome at times. Ruining lives. Ruining the air. Ruining the Earth. However, they shone so blindingly bright that even their prey would forgive them easily.

Enraged. Harsh and infuriated. Hatred filled the particles of this light. The mere presence of anything else would fill these beauties with animosity.

Animosity for what was; what could have been. Melancholy secretly resided with these rays. A bitter secret. A sour secret.

Combined-these rays, this moonlight…it was breath taking. People looked up to the night sky to search for them. To see them. To be part of the splendour.

They continued to glisten.

Glisten through ecstasy.

And still…I thrive

Your racist taunts can't bring me down.

As I will always wear the crown.

Here I am, on your table.

Sorry, I should say, 'our' table.

You struggle to cope.

Why is that?

Never seen a brown person on your 'level'?

Don't patronise me. It'll never work.

It's my turn now. You can't stop me

And yet still you try…

And still…I thrive.

Keepsake

I have so many scars from every single battle and war I have fought. Then I met you and stopped fighting. You made my heart skip a beat. You made me lose all rhythm and rhyme. You brought me safety. The warm embraces. The winter nights. The crunchy Autumn walks. Finding shade in the sun. I want to live in the embrace. Keep me there and never let go.

Purpose

Sleepless nights.

Agonising days.

Goals in mind.

I didn't come to play.

Aamir Dean Hassan

To Be Free

———✦———

Close your eyes and allow yourself to be...

...taken away....

Free　　　　　　Free

　　　Free　　　　　Free

The aim and goal

The ultimate

Not to escape

But to be...

　　　Free

Skin Deep

———❖———

Why can't I like what I see?

Why do I not look like the other men?

I see only dirt in the mirror.

Filthy and ugly brown skin.

Nobody wants this.

I want to rip out my insides and

smear them on my reflection.

Maybe then I can be appealing?

You aren't and will never be good enough.

You don't have the nerve, beauty or talents.

Nobody will ever want to hold you.

Nobody wants to feel your skin on theirs.

I shake my head and see black.

I need this Monster in my head to leave.

I fall because I am dizzy and

so sick of looking at my reflection.

I can't eat without abhorrence;

without being able to puke my insides out.

I blackout again and again

and fall into obscurity.

You are a waste of flesh and bone.

You deserve demise and to be buried without a tear.

Nobody will ever want to touch you.

I shake my head and see…

I see pictures on the wall.

These pictures resemble everything I want to be.

Tall, white and picture perfect.

I long to taste the splendor of love.

I long to be loved.

I long for my inner saboteur to disappear.

Can I Escape My Mind?

You will never find passion.

Nobody will ever love you.

I shake my head and see broken glass,

I reach out and I cut.

I cut so deep and relish the feeling.

Joy and self-love have arrived;

I finally feel alive

You will forever be undesirable.

My brown skin covered in carnage

It was never ever beautiful

I see the light slowly approaching

The world won't have to suffer anymore

Aamir Dean Hassan

Finally, you are gone.

Finally, the world is a better place.

My eyes flicker open.

I am still here.

I still live and breathe.

I see my brown skin in all

its pain and glory.

My brown skin makes me a Warrior.

My brown skin has History.

My brown skin is Power.

I am here and I stand strong.

I am here and I am glowing.

The voice in my mind dies.

My brown skin is the beauty that survives.

Lineage

They Are Here

---·❊·---

I finally feel them. I never knew I could feel such power and such energy.

My ancestors have given me their blessings.

Rip and tear through my soul, live, stampede, dance, fly through me…

It is all yours. Power through my vessel…

Bigger

We come together and talk with such mite and passion.

We sip our chai, smoke our shisha, smell the spices of our people.

We march, we feel, we connect.

This is true magic.

It's so special and beyond comprehension.

We are part of something so big and so special.

Something much bigger than you and I.

Just Smile

They will do anything in their power, abiding the laws of the land as much as they can, they will…anything to make you feel insignificant. To break you…

They are afraid of what you are. You are a King. You are THE Queen. Head up high. Stand up straight. Be ferocious but with a smile on your face. Do not let them take you to anger. Smile.

Smile and be free. Smile and feel the bold tormented strength of your lineage. Do this for them. They are here in your soul and in your spirit.

Motherland

Keep the jewels you stole. Keep everything you stole.

It was too powerful for your use and that is why we wanted to protect you from it.

Your greed knew no bounds. Savage is imprinted in your DNA.

You took it all and did what?

Created misery. No light. No love. No passion. No feeling.

And you continue to take, take, take.

Leave me. Leave my people be.

The power of love we hold is too strong and you can never take it.

My ancestors are here to see what you did, they laugh, and they pity you.

Message from my people:

Back to the Motherland we go.

Home

I am Aamir.

I am a Prince.

I come from Queens & Kings.

My riches know no bounds.

My riches live within me.

You can never break me.

Take me back to my Motherland.

Let me feel the ground beneath my feet.

Let me breathe the air of my people.

Let me decolonise every fiber of my being.

Let me be free of the tormented souls that have haunted and plagued my existence.

Devilish

―――✦―――

The embers burn of the spirit of our ancestors,

It's time to set the place on fire!

Our Power

We fought in the Battle of the Ten Kings

Vedic Sanskrit runs through my veins.

The fear this exudes is encapsulated in strength,

A foreign land to you, is the home within me.

The universe is whispering, follow the guidance to keep the balance.

With one look, we can evoke the fear of the son of Nyx.

With a touch, the mist of Erebos can be summoned.

My tribes are so mighty, and they stampede with fierce force.

My origin is so challenging to discover…

Bloodline: Pashtun

The essence of hundreds of tribes running through my body.

Magic hidden and concealed.

Magic, they tried to take. You could never take what lives within me…

Stand back and no harm shall be done.

Strike us and the spirits will cast their enchantments.

Free Mind

Awakened into Consciousness

Awakened.

Finally

Unconscious? Not anymore.

Only when you are present do you see you have been assimilating in the matrix for so long.

The universe woke me up.

The trip woke me up.

I am finally here, time to have the time of my life.

Universe

The presence I needed is here,

And I shall be keeping it close forever.

Your thoughts may subside into misery, ocean deep,

But your mind is now strong enough to bring you back before you drown.

Does this mean I will never drown again?

No. It means you know adversity brings strength. Adversity makes you stronger.

The process of healing is at super speed. You are needed in this world.

A Path Not Too Far

Have you found your purpose?

Take a stroll with me…I've found mine.

I have the Key to the Kingdom of your mind and soul.

I have the Key to unlock what is beyond.

You do not have to go far as it all lives here within you.

Breathe.

Breathe.

Breathe.

Let the universe guide you to your purpose.

Pay your respects by fulfilling your duty.

Presence

Presence is your most powerful tool,

to know you are living truly and only for you.

To know the external doesn't matter,

all that matters is you in the universe at this moment.

Present.

Remain present.

You can be happy wherever you are.

The river will try to drown you from time to time

but you shall remain in the moment and

continue to save yourself from ever drowning again.

Presence is your most powerful tool.

Evolution

Forgive your formerly unconscious soul.

for all it had done to harm yourself and inflict

revenge on others.

You have evolved.

You are now kind, caring, free and happy.

You are now spiritual, humble, calm and light.

The new you may be hard to comprehend

but you know you belong to the world and beyond.

Your intentions are pure.

That's all that matters.

Magic

———✧———

Drowning in tears of happiness every single day.

Full of gratitude to be an explorer on this planet.

A spiritual being having a human experience.

Allowing nature to overwhelm me.

Leaving those who wish to harm me alone.

Feeling the fabrics of the galaxies in my fingertips.

Magic.

In disbelief you are here…shake it off…you are here!

Thank you to the version of me willing to push to get here.

Through the hardship and hurt came brilliance.

Magic.

Thank You

Thank you, Universe.

For the pain and adversity.

Thank you, Universe.

For bestowing your blessings on to me.

Thank you, Universe.

For all you are going to bring me.

Thank you, Universe…

INKFEATHERS PUBLISHING

www.inkfeathers.com

We love creating beautiful books for you!

Come be a part of our ever-growing community of authors. Grow, write, and publish with us!

Scan here to explore books, authors and more

Connect with us on socials. We'd love to hear from you!

f 🐦 in 📷   Inkfeathers Publishing